THE DEEP STATE AND ITS AGENDA FOR HUMANITY

A Christian view of history

Dr Ali Ansarifar

Disclaimer

It has never been the intention of the author of this book to infringe on the sensitivity, personal faith, or beliefs of his readers. The material and information presented in this book are never meant to cause offence to any individual person or group of people of any race, nationality, religion, or background. This book is written for educational purposes and academic interest only.

Kingdom Publishers

Copyright© Dr Ali Ansarifar 2025

All rights reserved. No part of this book may be reproduced in any form by photocopying or any electronic or mechanical means, including information storage or retrieval systems, without permission in writing from both the copyright owner and the publisher of the book. The right of Dr Ali Ansarifar to be identified as the author of this work has been asserted by him in accordance with the Copyright, Designs, and Patents Act 1988 and any subsequent amendments thereto.

A catalogue record for this book is available from the British Library.

All Scripture quotations have been taken from The Interlinear Hebrew-Greek-English version of the Bible

ISBN: 978-1-916801-29-5

1st Edition 2025 by Kingdom Publishers, London, UK.

You can purchase copies of this book from any leading bookstore or at:
www.kingdompublishers.co.uk

Dedication

I dedicate this book to those who strive to make the world a better place to live and to the glory of God the Father through our Lord Jesus Christ.

Table of Contents

Dedication	4
Preface	6
Chapter 1 The wars in heaven, hunter-gatherers and the beginning of human civilisations	15
Chapter 2 The rise of empires and the start of human bondage	21
Chapter 3 The deep state and its agenda for humanity	29
Chapter 4 The Battle of Armageddon	37
Chapter 5 Summary and conclusions	42
References	56
Afterword	60
About the author	61
About the book	62
Final notes by the author	63
Books by the author	64

Preface

The rise of civilisations and the ability to manage them well is one of the greatest achievements of humankind. However, when civilisations become the engines of empires, they transform the empires into highly efficient and rigid systems of bondage from which humankind can never escape. In the last 5,000 years, there have been more than 200 empires. Some empires lasted for a few years, and many others lasted for over two millennia. There is no doubt that empires have contributed a great deal to human progress and well-being, but they have also caused some adverse impacts on human societies, which to this day are causing divisions and mayhem in the world. For example, racism, militarism, human trafficking and slavery, conquest, pillage, the annihilation of cultures and cultural heritage, and global wars, to mention a few. All empires, with no exception, decline and fall into decay after rising to power and gaining glory. The fall of empires curtails their excesses and limits the appetite and desires of their leaders to acquire more wealth and power, as well as the subjugation of people by the force of arms. But how can humanity be freed from the clutches of the empires? The Bible tells us that the Lord God liberated a people from slavery and made a covenant with them to transform them into a model nation, and by doing so, he strived to free humankind from the bondage of the forces of history. However, this plan had to be revised because the dark forces operating within the empires were too powerful to be overcome by demanding monotheism and imposing rigid moral law, as God intended to do through the covenant with His people. The pagan Roman Empire adopted

Christianity, and this resulted in the establishment of the Papacy and the Catholic Church. The Papacy persecuted the Jews for over a millennium, and this led to the birth of Zionism and the creation of the State of Israel in the Middle East in the late 19th and the mid-20th century, respectively. Zionism acts as a portal for the dark forces of history that are shaping human affairs and preparing the world for a final act of rebellion against God. The kingdom of God will come after the empire's end. The State of Israel is the final resting place of the Zionist portal. History will end after a third temple is built in Jerusalem, where the man of sin will sit and claim to be God, demanding to be worshipped, and then Jesus will return. For now, events are moving rapidly towards a global conflict where all eyes will focus on a false Messiah, the man of sin, who will allegedly save the world and bring peace to humanity. The battle between the forces of light and darkness will take place on a global stage. The unfolding events will soon engulf the world in major conflicts and great upheaval, the likes of which humanity has never experienced before in its entire history. A Christian view of history will help to understand the context in which events are unfolding.

The idea that humans can influence and shape the processes in history and the unfolding events is foolish. History is reaching a conclusion that was created by the events of the dawn of time.

The welcome party of Satan on Earth is ungodliness, inhumanity, lawlessness, cruelty, hate, lies, bloodshed, immorality, and denial. Everything is ready for the master of darkness to arrive.

Jesus Christ will greet the righteous in the bridal chamber. The unjust have already been in the chamber of their own indignation, but they don't yet realise it.

An examination of biblical history asserts that God is impersonal. But human wisdom denies this assertion and resorts to old fables. Where is the truth?

Human relationships with gods in pre-Abrahamic religions were based on fear, ignorance, superstition, and blood sacrifices. The Abrahamic religions are linked to the Crusades, antisemitism, and Jihad. Where is godliness?

He who has the truth.

Jesus said, "I shall give you what eyes have not seen, what ears have not heard, what hands have not touched, what has not come upon the human heart." [1]

A Christian view of history

Angelic rebellion in heaven and the rise of Satan and the fallen angels.

↓

The emergence of a Satanic spirit of rebellion, ungodliness, and hate (deep state).

↓

Angelic interference in human affairs and the birth of the giants.

↓

The corruption of humankind and the great flood.

↓

The destruction of the giants and the rise of demons.

↓

The coupling of the deep state with the rise and fall of the world's empires.

↓

The Christianisation of the pagan Roman Empire and the emergence of the anti-Christ.

↓

The birth of Zionism and the opening of a portal to the deep state.

↓

The rebuilding of the Third Temple in Jerusalem and the rise of the Satanically-inspired man of sin.

↓

The destruction of the man of sin and the return of Jesus Christ.

↓

The end of the age.

Chapter 1
The wars in heaven, hunter-gatherers and the beginning of human civilisations

In the story of humankind, the beginning is a story of its own, and the verses in Genesis 1:3-5 in the Bible provide a fascinating reading. At the dawn of time, God separated light from darkness to produce duality. The forces of darkness were violent and destructive, whereas the forces of light were creative and constructive. The duality of light and darkness provided a medium in which all creatures—plants, animals, and humans—came into existence of their own accord despite immense struggle and unimaginably destructive processes and filled the Earth. However, the forces of darkness adversely affected God's creation, causing angelic rebellion and human disobedience to God's commands that corrupted the angelic world and humanity. This was the beginning of human servitude to the hostile forces of history.

The war in the heavens and the angelic rebellion

It all started when light (God) came into existence of its own accord. [1] God then separated light from darkness to produce duality, from which the world was made. (Genesis 1:4-5) In the days when God created the angels, there was a great war in heaven. Lucifer, known also as the son of the morning, wanted to ascend into heaven and exalt himself above the stars of God. He desired to be like God. He assembled one-third of the angels in heaven and waged war. Michael and his host fought against Lucifer and his army, and Michael prevailed. Lucifer was thrown down to the Earth in defeat and dishonour. Lucifer, whose name became Satan, the devil, and Mastema, was wicked and became the hater of all that is good. According to the Bible, Adam and Eve were the first male and female humans that God created. Lucifer thought to himself, "God has promised salvation to Adam by covenant and promised that He would deliver him from all the hardships that have befallen him, but God has not promised me by covenant and will not deliver me out of my hardships. He has promised Adam that He would make him and his descendants live in the kingdom that I once lived in. I will kill Adam. The Earth shall get rid of him. The Earth shall be left to me alone. When he is dead, he will not have any descendants left to inherit the kingdom and it will remain my own realm. God will then be wanting me, and He will restore it to me and my hosts." [2] This was a declaration of war on God and humanity by Satan and his fallen angels, who have remained a potent destructive force in human affairs ever since and seek to corrupt and destroy the children of man. The defeat and expulsion of Lucifer and the fallen angels from heaven gave rise to a spirit of ungodliness, rebellion, lawlessness, and hate (the Spirit of Wickedness)that has persisted in the universe and corrupted all aspects of God's creation. The Spirit has had a profoundly adverse influence on humanity and its relationship with God.

In the troublesome history of humankind, there have been events in the past that have had a profound impact on the destiny of the world. After God created the angels, he appointed the Watchers to watch over men. They were to instruct the children of men to do justice and be upright. The children of men multiplied, and beautiful and fair daughters were born to them. And the angels, the sons of heaven, saw and lusted after them, each choosing one for himself, defiled themselves with sex with them, and had children with them. The daughters of men gave birth, and the offspring of the angels were giants who populated the Earth. The giants were profoundly evil and immoral, performed dreadful deeds and gross sinful sexual acts on male and female humans and animals, and made offensive discourse. They devoured and sacrificed the animals and sought to devour humans; they committed injustice and shed much blood; and the Earth was filled with sin. As a result, all the Earth grew more corrupt. As degeneracy and immoral conduct continued among the giants and humans, God destroyed all wrong from the face of the Earth, ended every evil work through a flood, and prepared the world for the righteous men to live. The flood destroyed all flesh, but the spirits of the giants, the evil ones, were not destroyed. The disembodied spirit of the giants sought out the flesh of animals and humans in which to live after their bodies were destroyed in the flood. However, after the flood, the spirits of the evil ones, or the demons, continued to inhabit animal and human flesh once more. [2]

After the wars in heaven, fallen angels and demons appeared and affected the lives of humans. These entities serve the forces of darkness and torment humanity. The Bible teaches that humanity is not wrestling against flesh and blood but against the rulers, against the authorities, against the rulers of this world, against the darkness of this age, against the spiritual powers of evil in the heavenlies. (Ephesians 6:11-12) Satan and his hosts constitute the deep state. In the scheme of human salvation, emancipation from the deep state or the spiritual forces of evil has been a central theme. In his ministry, Jesus cast out a demon from a tormented man and freed him from the clutches of demonic possession. (Mark 1:21-28) The destruction of the deep state has been one of God's goals in His plan for human salvation, and this was achieved by the birth, ministry, and ascension of Jesus Christ to heaven, the Christianisation of the Roman Empire, and antisemitism. These topics will be examined in detail later in this book.

The rise of human societies and the world's civilisations

The early primitive human societies started with hunting and gathering. This demanded a significant degree of mobility among humans in search of suitable animals and places to hunt them. Then, the development of food production through organised farming provided an effective method for humans to multiply and civilisations to emerge. Grain cultivation was an important step in the development of agriculture, and it spread into Europe and other places such as India, Africa, and China. [3]

However, after agriculture dominated the lives of the early humans, complex and skilled societies that we call civilisations emerged much later in various places around the globe at different speeds of expansion and sophistication. For a small society to develop into a civilisation and for a civilised people to survive, food production had to remain uninterrupted, and this required efficient irrigation to ensure that the land produced rich crops for harvesting year after year from the same fields. When irrigation was needed, large numbers of men cooperated in preparing the land, for example, by digging and diking. This required good organisation and the development of appropriate skills and know-how, and eventually, agricultural surplus helped to support and expand the skilled humans and their social organisation. One major flaw was dependence on irrigation. If irrigation was disrupted for a sufficiently long period of time, food production would have ceased, and famine would have resulted. [3]

The introduction of animals to the tasks of cultivation, the invention of some basic technologies such as the plough, and the extension of agriculture to rain-watered land helped farmers increase food production very significantly and produce an agricultural surplus, as had previously been possible in irrigation farming. A distinctive social order was put in place to compel the farmers to hand over their surplus crops to their rulers to support the construction of new courts and palace cities. [3]

As agricultural societies spread, and more complex social orders were established, events in other parts of the world started to have a major impact on human lives. Pastoralists and warriors from the steppe managed to tame horses and use them to arm their chariots for warfare. Having perfected techniques for warfare, they then moved to the fringes of the civilised world, overran, and conquered the populated areas and the peasants in agricultural lands. The interaction between the pre-existing agricultural people and the new masters of the land led to the development of new civilisations in Europe, India, and China. In the Middle East, the civilised nations that were skilled in chariot-based warfare competed for supremacy. But the barbarian invasion defeated these empires, and new empires arose under the Assyrians and the Persians. This merger led to the emergence of a new cosmopolitan Middle East and the rise of Judaism. Before the end of the sixth century, the Buddhism of India, the Confucianism of China, and the philosophy of Greece were highly influential, shaping the lives of their followers. [3] The structures required for the rise of more advanced societies and civilisations such as the Babylonian, Medo-Persian, Greek, and Roman were in place, and this has been one of the greatest achievements of humankind. But when the civilisations are captured by empire builders and their leaders and their resources are utilised for waging wars of conquest and enslavement of the masses, they become an instrument of bondage. Then a cycle of devastation results from the rise and fall of empires, which humankind has never managed to overcome to this day. This topic will be discussed in more detail in the next chapter.

Summary

• The angelic rebellion in heaven produced Satan and the fallen angels. This constitutes a Satanically-inspired spirit of rebellion, ungodliness, and hate that serves the intentions and schemes of the dark forces of the universe and influences human behaviour, events, and the destiny of humankind adversely.

• The angelic interference in human affairs led to the birth of the giants and the corruption of humankind. The great flood destroyed the giants, causing disembodied spirits known as demons or evil spirits to emerge and torment humans. Satan, the fallen angels, and the demons are the "deep state" through which the dark forces of the universe oppose God and humanity.

In the next chapter, the author proposes that the empires have provided a home for the deep state to enslave humanity and keep it in bondage. Four major empires in history—Babylonian, Medo-Persian, Greek, and Roman—that are mentioned in the Bible will be examined briefly. There can be no salvation for humanity unless this bondage is broken, and humans are freed from its dreadful clutches.

Chapter 2
The rise of empires and the start of human bondage

The history of humankind is littered with great achievements and disastrous failures. The rise and fall of empires have been the driving force behind the processes of history that have brought us to the modern age. The empires of Babylon, Medo-Persia, Greece, and Rome have a unique place in God's providence for the salvation of humankind. After the Babylonian invasion of the Holy Land, the Jewish and gentile worlds merged, and the destiny of the Jews was linked with the rise and fall of the Babylonian, Medo-Persian, Greek, and Roman Empires.

The merger of the Jewish and gentile worlds

There have been various empires in history, but the exact number is not known. During the last four thousand years, there have been at least 200 empires, some lasting for as short as 1 year and some others for as long as 2060 years. [4] The Babylonian, Medo-Persian, Greek, and Roman Empires have had, at times, very difficult relationships with the Jews over millennia, which led to their displacement and persecution. The merger of the Jewish and gentile worlds after the Babylonian invasion of the Holy Land is of major importance in understanding current events and God's providence for saving humanity. But first, the history of these four empires will be reviewed briefly.

The Babylonian Empire- The Babylonian Empire (1792-1595 BC) [5] was in an ancient region between the Tigris and Euphrates rivers. Today, it is an area from around Baghdad to the Persian Gulf that was first settled about 4000 BCE before Babylon rose to political importance at about 1850 BCE. The region had a rich civilisation that pioneered the first system of writing, the earliest known codes of law, the development of the city-state, the invention of the potter's wheel, the sailboat, and the seed plough, and the creation of literary, musical, and architectural forms. The Empire was engaged in a series of wars, and a new line of kings emerged, one of whom was Nebuchadnezzar II. King Nebuchadnezzar invaded and conquered the Kingdom of Judah in 587 BCE, destroyed the First Temple in Jerusalem, which was built by King Solomon, and burned down the city. He deported prominent citizens and a sizable portion of the Jewish population of Judah from the land into exile and dispersed them throughout his empire. In 539 BCE, the Persian king Cyrus the Great conquered Babylon, and the Babylonian Empire came under Persian control. [6,7]

The Achaemenid Persian Empire - The Achaemenid Persian Empire (550-330 BCE) was created by nomadic Persians. It was based in the south-western portion of the Iranian Plateau in the region of Persis, and Persepolis was its official capital. [8] Its territory stretched from the Balkans and Eastern Europe in the west to the Indus Valley in the east. The Empire created a cosmopolitan society by assimilating people of various races and faiths and contributing a great deal to the creation of a civil society. It developed an effective method for running centralised bureaucratic administration for building infrastructure for the postal and road systems, enforced the use of an official language for all its citizens, and trained and maintained a large professional army. [9] The Empire conducted major military campaigns during its expansion. The Persian-Babylonian wars, led by Cyrus between 547 BCE and 539 BCE, defeated the Babylonian Empire. Cyrus emancipated the people of Judah from their exile and ordered the restoration of Jerusalem and the Second Temple. The famous "Cyrus Declaration" allowed the Jews who were living in exile by the river of Babylon to return to their homeland, Judea, to rebuild their lives. But some who had established themselves economically and socially preferred to remain on Babylonian-Persian soil. The tolerant attitude of the rulers towards Jewish subjects brought gratitude from the Jews and found expression in subsequent generations. The Talmud says a picture of Susa, the capital of the Persian kings, should be carved on the eastern gate of the temple in Jerusalem. Many scholars say this was intended in memory of good relations with Persia's Achaemenid kings. [10] The Persian army sacked Athens between 480 and 479 BCE, but some years later, the Greeks defeated the Persians and destroyed their empire. [11]

The Greek Empire - The Greek Empire was established in 300 BCE, when Alexander the Great united small city-states under one rule. The Empire stretched into Europe, Egypt, and south-west Asia. [12] Under Alexander the Great, the Greeks waged wars of conquest and conversion. They expanded their control into Egypt and India, conquered Babylon, defeated the Persian Empire in 331 BCE, and set its capital, Persepolis, on fire. They also founded the great city of Alexandria in Egypt, which became a centre of learning. [13] The Greeks made advances in geography and the natural sciences and took the major centres of civilisation eastward. Some aspects of Hellenistic culture, such as the Greek language and coinage, strengthened the trading and cultural networks in the world. Alexander the Great died in 323 BCE, and his empire was divided into the Ptolemaic Kingdom of Egypt, the Seleucid Empire in the east, the Kingdom of Pergamon in Asia Minor, and Macedon. [14] Judea was a part of the Ptolemaic Kingdom and Seleucid Empire around 200 BCE and was governed by the Hasmonean dynasty. The Maccabean dynasty is often used as a replacement for the entire Hasmonean dynasty. Judea was heavily Hellenized, resulting in a struggle between Judaism and Hellenism and a revolt. In 166 BCE, Judah Maccabee led an army to victory over the Seleucid dynasty, destroyed Hellenizing Jews and pagan altars in the villages, and forced Jews into outlawry. After victory was secured, the Maccabees captured Jerusalem, cleansed the Second Temple, and re-established Jewish worship. Judea remained under the control of the Seleucid Empire until 129 BCE. The Hasmoneans ruled it until 63 BCE, when it became a client kingdom of Rome. This period of martyrs and heroic military leaders saved Judaism from annihilation and Israel from its enemies. [15]

The Roman Empire - The Roman Empire (27–395 AD) - The Roman Republic was founded in 509 BCE and ended in 27 BCE. It expanded into an empire through wars and military conquest under the dictatorial rule of the Caesars, who secured territories stretching from the Atlantic to the Caspian Sea and from Britain to the Sahara. The Empire expanded, new people were made Roman citizens, and new cults and religions were tolerated and integrated into the pantheon of Roman gods. [16] However, nationalism and friction between different religious belief systems, as well as issues related to taxation, caused discontent and led to rebellion within the Empire. The Roman Republic conquered Judea in 63 BCE, and it remained a Roman province from 6 to 132 AD. The demand on the monotheistic Jews to worship the emperor, coupled with systematic discrimination and the burden of heavier taxes, led to the Jewish revolt in Judaea between 66 AD and 70 AD. The wrath of the Roman military machine was unleashed on the Temple complex, and the

Romans broke into the holiest of the holy, slaughtered every Jew, and looted whatever they could put their hands on, including gold and silver and the most precious religious relics. The city of Judea pillaged, burned, and was razed to the ground, and the rebellion came to a bloody end with over one million dead and thousands of prisoners delivered into slavery. After years of military conquest and expansion and 700 years of rule, the Western Roman Empire started its slow decline, and by 476 AD, it broke into small kingdoms governed by barbarians and fell into the Dark Ages. In 312 CE, the Roman Empire adopted Christianity as its formal religion. [16] This event laid the foundation for the revival of the Empire into a modern papacy under the Popes of the Roman Catholic Church.

The Jews in Babylon - When the Jews were in exile in Babylon, King Nebuchadnezzar had a dream which upset him greatly. He dreamed of an image. That great image stood before him with a brilliant brightness and its form was dreadful. The head of the image was gold; its breasts and arms were of silver; its belly and its thighs were of bronze; its legs were of iron; its feet were partly of iron and partly of clay. A stone was cut out without hands, which struck the image on its feet of iron and clay and broke them to pieces. Then the iron, the clay, the bronze, the silver, and the gold were together broken to pieces; and they became like the chaff of the summer threshing floors. And the wind carried them away, so that no trace was found for them. And the stone that struck the image became a great mountain and filled the whole Earth. The head of gold represents the Babylonian Empire; the chest and arms of silver represent the Medo-Persian Empire; the belly and thighs of bronze represent the Greek Empire; and the legs of iron represent the Roman Empire. The feet partly of Iron and partly of clay represent a divided kingdom that would be partly strong and partly brittle. A stone not cut by human hands which strikes the statue on its feet and destroys it represents an eternal kingdom by God that will last forever. (Daniel 2:31-35)

The Babylonian invasion of the Holy Land and the exile of the Jews in Babylon merged the Jewish and gentile worlds. This enabled God to condition the processes of history to put the rising empires of Medo-Persia, Greece, and Rome on a trajectory to end this age. The destiny of the Jews or Israel was interwoven entirely with the occurring events and circumstances inside these empires and no longer by God or the covenant He made with their ancestors. Israel became the cornerstone of God's plan to end the reign of the empires. This topic will be revisited in Chapter 3.

Empires have risen to power and glory through invasion, conquest, subjugation, exploitation, and transferring wealth and labour from the conquered nations through the militarisation and projection of excessive force. This has led to unimaginable suffering and bloodshed. For example, in the first Roman Jewish war, 1.2 million non-combatants and 25,000–30,000 soldiers died. [17] In the 20th century, 231 million people died in conflicts caused by clashes between empires and national states. [17] The landscape of the world's empires is littered with dead and injured humans, devastated cities and villages, shattered dreams, bitter disappointment, and misery. The empires have caused significant upheaval in human societies and impacted human lives adversely. Racial stereotyping and racism; militarism; human trafficking and slavery; drug trade; immoral acquisition of other people's land and wealth; global wars and bloodshed; conquest; pillage; population reduction; destruction to farmland, water irrigation systems, and agriculture; imposed starvation and disease on civilian populations; annihilation of cultures and cultural heritage have been a plague on humanity. [18] Humanity has benefited a great deal from the contributions the empires have made to its progress and wellbeing, but war sweeps aside all these benefits and gains and leaves desolation behind. The evidence is obvious to see in the modern age. All the indications are that the deep state is rooted in the rise and fall of the world's empires, and humanity is in bondage to it. The salvation of humanity will depend on breaking this bondage and destroying the forces behind it. The question is, "How can this be achieved?" Some verses in Genesis 1 in the Bible provide the answer. These verses will be visited in the next chapter.

Summary

- The emergence of advanced societies and civilisations provided humanity with the skills, abundant resources, continuity, and stability that are essential for progress. However, they also provided fertile ground for the rise of empires, with calamitous consequences following their collapse.

- Empires use the force of arms, extreme violence, and bloodshed to capture the rich resources of civilisations and turn them into tools for the invasion, conquest, subjugation, pillaging of citizens, and the transfer and acquisition of foreign labour and resources. This serves the desires, inspirations, and greed of the empire builders, not the ordinary people.

- The fall of the empires has caused the displacement, destitution, and destruction of countless numbers of people. The benefits that the empires offer to humanity are swept away when the empires collapse from within or are destroyed by foreign invasion.

- Empires have provided the deep state with an ideal setting to enslave humanity and keep it in bondage. For humanity to have any future, this bondage must be broken, and humanity emancipated.

- The merger of the Jewish and gentile worlds after the Babylonian invasion was essential in defeating the deep state and liberating humankind from the bondage. However, further steps were needed to end the reign of the world's empires. This will be discussed in the next chapter.

Chapter 3
The deep state and its agenda for humanity

In the scheme of Providence, God's work in the person of Jesus Christ has unique importance. Since the act of creation took place in the duality of light and darkness, nothing can exist outside of this dualism. However, dualism corrupted all aspects of God's creation and the created order, including humanity. Hence, this dictated that emancipation from duality was essential before God's plan for human salvation could be realised. The forces of darkness are a potent force and deeply hostile to God and humanity. The angelic rebellion in heaven served the power of darkness and became its agency. This hostile power and its hosts are rooted in the rise and fall of the world's empires and have kept humanity in bondage. In Jesus Christ, the duality was dissolved, and the hostile powers were defeated, liberating humans from their clutches. Now all that remains is for the hostile powers to incarnate into a human form and be destroyed in the second coming of Jesus Christ. The incarnation will take place within a historical framework set by God through the birth, ministry, and resurrection of Jesus Christ, and Jerusalem will be the epicentre of this cosmic event.

When God separated light from darkness, dualism emerged. In dualism, all things came into existence by their accords through an immense struggle, competition, and destruction. The wonderful world of plants, animals, and humans that exists today is the product of this creative but flawed dualism. Soon after light and darkness were separated, angels were created, most of whom obeyed, but some disobeyed God's command and rebelled. Dualism dictates that whatever comes into existence must have its opposite. For example, obedience and disobedience, good and bad, honest and dishonest, perfect and flawed, beauty and ugliness, and life and death. On this basis, Christ had to have the opposite, the anti-Christ. The Roman Catholic Church has produced some of the greatest saints in the history of Christianity. [19] However, as history reveals, it also has a dark side, which led to the wars of the Crusades against millions of non-Christian and Christian people. [20] Since Christ is present in the Catholic Church, it may be concluded that the anti-Christ must be present too, because dualism dictates so. As discussed in Chapter 2, the deep state is rooted in the world's empires, and the anti-Christ is its agent in the Catholic Church. There are some other indicators to support this claim.

The Christianisation of the Roman Empire

As mentioned before, when God separated between light and darkness, He created duality, in which all His creative works appeared over a very long time. (Genesis 1:4-5) In this duality, opposites emerged: obedience and disobedience; good and bad; belief and disbelief; honesty and dishonesty; curses and blessings; kindness and cruelty; life and death. All things came into existence by their accords in the duality of light and darkness, and everything has an opposite. [1] Nothing can happen outside of dualism. God's covenant with ancient Israel demanded strict monotheism and commanded full obedience to His moral law. This violated dualism and could never have succeeded. Dualism dictates that monotheism must couple with its opposite, polytheism and morality with its opposite, immorality. No divine command or punishment can change it.

When the pagan Roman Empire was Christianised, and the Catholic Church established, Christ was introduced into the Empire, and the opposite, the anti-Christ, emerged in the Church, as dictated by dualism. So, God conditioned the Empire to have Christ and anti-Christ. While God works through Christ to bring salvation, Satan works through the anti-Christ to do the opposite. Since in duality all things will end, and nothing can escape its destructive power, a process was in place to end the reign of the empires. In the final act, the Satanically-inspired forces of the anti-Christ must be destroyed. For the final battle of Armageddon, Satan and his hosts that are in a different dimension must descend to Earth, and for that to happen, they must come through a portal and couple with the incarnated man of sin who will sit in the Third Temple in Jerusalem to claim to be God. (2 Thessalonians 2:3–10) But what is the portal, and where is it?

When Rome adopted Christianity as the religion of the Empire, the Jews were heavily persecuted because of antisemitism, and this led to the birth of Zionism sometime in the late 18th century. [20] Since the birth of Zionism, three major events in the 19th and 20th centuries have shaped the world we know today. The Bolshevik revolution in Russia, the Jewish Holocaust in Europe, and the creation of the State of Israel in Palestine have had far-reaching repercussions for humanity. A close examination of these events suggests that since the birth of Zionism the deep state has had a direct hand in shaping these historical events.

The Roman and Byzantine Empires

The Byzantine Empire (395–1453 BCE) was the eastern half of the Roman Empire and lasted for a thousand years after the western part collapsed. The Greek East and Latin West of the Roman Empire diverged sometime between the 3rd and 6th centuries after Constantinople was established as its capital by Constantine in 330 AD. The new empire adopted Christianity as the state religion. [21] Despite sharing Christianity as their religion, in 1054 AD, schism damaged the relationship between Constantinople and the Holy See (the Catholic Church or the Latin Church). The schism, known also as the Great Schism, broke the communion of the Western and Eastern Christians, who were a part of the Universal Catholic Church, into the Western Roman Catholic Church and the Eastern Orthodox Church, respectively. The relationship between the two never recovered and led to military conflict and the defeat of the Byzantine Empire. [22] The Latin Church waged a series of religious wars against the Muslims to secure control of holy sites that were considered sacred by both groups. The Fourth Crusade was a Latin Christian armed expedition to recapture Muslim-controlled Jerusalem. [20] In 1204 AD, the Latin Church launched the Fourth Crusade. The initial goal was the re-establishment of Christian rule over Jerusalem. But instead, it captured and sacked the capital of Byzantium. [22,23] The conquest fragmented the Byzantine Empire, contributed to its decline, killed thousands of its soldiers, depleted its resources, people, and money, and left the region vulnerable to attack. The Empire finally succumbed to the Ottomans in 1453 AD. The Latin Church has remained antagonistic towards the Orthodox Church and is mainly responsible for the demise of the Byzantine Empire. After the defeat, the centre of Orthodox Christianity was moved to Moscow, Russia, in the 14th century. [24]

The Catholic Church and the Jews

As mentioned, the Crusades waged by the Catholic Church were religious wars between Christians and Muslims to secure control of holy sites considered sacred by both groups. There were eight major crusades, which started in 1096 AD and ended in 1291 AD. The persecution of the Jews started in the first Crusade and continued for centuries. Although Jews were previously persecuted mainly by plundering them, the Crusades aimed at annihilating them. The Jews were labelled as Christ-killers and had to embrace the Cross or die. Millions of Muslims and Jews lost their lives. The Crusaders rationalised the killing of the Jews as an extension of their Catholic mission. The persecution of the Jews included massacres, expulsions, confiscation of properties and possessions, heavy taxation, forced conversion, book burnings, desecration of the holy religious places, and slavery, culminating in the Holocaust in the 20th century, where 6 million Jews were killed. The Second Vatican Council, or Vatican II, between 1962 and 1965 repudiated charges of deicide against the Jews and decried antisemitism in any form. However, the Council did uphold that the Jewish authorities and those who followed the lead pressed for the death of Christ; this could not be charged against all the Jews, without distinction, then alive, nor against the Jews of today.[25] This declaration ended two millennia of institutionalised antisemitism against Jews.

The Roman Catholic Church has had difficult relationship with the Orthodox Christians and Jews throughout its history. This led to the weakening and destruction of the Byzantine Empire and the death of countless Jews. But how were these relationships affected in the period after 1897, when Zionism was established?

The Bolsheviks revolution in Russia and the Jewish holocaust

It is believed that Christianity was introduced into Russia by Greek missionaries from Byzantium in the 9th century and was accepted as the state religion in 988. The Marxist-Leninist Bolshevik revolution of 1917 had a devastating effect on Russia. It destroyed the Tsarist state and transformed a democratic workers' state into a bureaucratic monstrosity, which was the Soviet Union. [26] The Soviet government declared the separation of church and state and nationalised all church-held lands. This was followed by the most brutal state-sanctioned persecutions, which included the extensive destruction of the churches and the arrest and execution of clerics. The church survived further upheaval under the communist party, and in around 1980, it started to recover after the Soviet Union collapsed and is now playing a major role in the lives of the Russian people. [24,27] It is believed that over 50 million people lost their lives under the Soviet system. [28]

When the National Socialist movement came to power in Germany in 1933 and founded the Third Reich, the leaders declared that the German nation was involved in a remorseless struggle—nation against nation, culture against culture, and ultimately race against race. There was a hierarchy of races, and the Aryans were the most valuable race. If Aryans were bred with people of inferior racial stock, their blood would be hopelessly polluted, and the Aryan race would gradually descend into extinction. It was claimed that the situation in Germany was critical and that drastic measures were needed to stop this defilement of Aryan blood. This was presented to the people of Germany as the historic mission of the National Socialist Movement. The greatest threat to Aryan purity was posed by the

Jews. The Jews were engaged in a global conspiracy to undermine existing states and cultures and to seize power. Judeo-Bolshevism in the Soviet Union was the greatest external threat to Germany. This laid down a pretext for the annihilation of the Jews and the Holocaust. In 1941, Nazi Germany invaded the Soviet Union, causing the deaths of an estimated 27 million civilians and military personnel. The mass murder of the Jews through mass shootings, deportations to extermination camps, and forced labour started in late 1941. The total number of Jews exterminated by the Nazis is estimated to be around six million. [29] The Balfour Declaration of 1917 and the Holocaust led to the creation of the State of Israel in the Middle East in 1948. [30] There is a momentum within some orthodox religious groups in Israel to rebuild the Third Temple in Jerusalem.

As discussed above, the Catholic Church has been responsible for the persecution of Jews and Orthodox Christians throughout most of its history. After the birth of Zionism, the persecution and enmity against the Jews and the Orthodox Christians persisted through racial stereotyping and atheistic communism, respectively, with a calamitous outcome for both people. The question is: what organisation was responsible for the persecution of Jews and Orthodox Christians in the post-Zionist period? The answer must be the Catholic Church, where the anti-Christ is. Zionism opened a portal to the deep state to enter and shape world affairs to pave the way for the incarnation of the anti-Christ into the man of sin. The main objective was to create a condition that forced Jews to return to Palestine to establish the State of Israel, where the Third Temple will be rebuilt. This was achieved through atheistic communism and race-versus-race struggle and competition, which were ungodly, highly destructive, and Satanic. The Catholic Church's historical hostility to the Orthodox Christians and Jews that extended into the post-Zionist period led to the creation of the State of Israel.

The deep state oversees world events, and we do well to remember that the end goal is to wipe humanity off this planet. For now, the State of Israel depends on continuous support from Britain and the United States for its survival. However, there must come a time when this support will disappear and Europe, with the aid of the Catholic Church, will take control of the fate of Israel. And when the Third Temple is rebuilt, the anti-Christ incarnates into the man of sin and sits in the Temple, demanding to be worshipped as God. Jesus will then return. Major global conflicts and hardships are on their way to force humanity to seek a saviour, who will be the devil himself.

Summary

• Historically, the Catholic Church has had conflicts with Jews and Orthodox Christians. This culminated in the wars of the Crusades and antisemitism. These conflicts continued in the 20th century after the birth of Zionism and were more destructive and led to the decimation of Orthodox Christians in Russia and Jews in the Holocaust in Europe. These long conflicts have resulted in the creation of the State of Israel in the Middle East. It can be argued that the deep state has been actively reshaping the landscape of human activities and world events through the anti-Christ in the Catholic Church and is paving the way for the coming of the man of sin.

• In the coming years, the Catholic Church will take a more active role in the world's affairs through a new European political and religious union, particularly in relation to the State of Israel, where the place will be prepared for the coming of the man of sin. The Vatican and Jerusalem will bring the long and tiresome human history to an end.

Chapter 4
The Battle of Armageddon

The brilliant, bright, and dreadful image that stood before King Nebuchadnezzar of Babylon and Daniel the prophet, interpreted as having the Babylonian Empire as its head, the Medo-Persian Empire as its chest and arms of silver, the Greek Empire as its belly and thighs of bronze, and the Roman Empire as its legs of iron, merits further scrutiny. In the image, the Roman Empire has legs, but the feet have not yet been formed. How will the feet form? Zionism and the State of Israel are setting the scene for the coming of the man of sin and the battle of Armageddon.

The role of Zionism and the State of Israel in the end times

When Jesus preached the gospel of salvation, some Jews accepted his message, and some rejected it. As a result, Israel was divided into two sects. One became the Church, and the other continued to adhere to Judaism and reject Christ. The former led to redemption, and the latter led to Zionism and the creation of the State of Israel. This division formed the legs of the Roman Empire in the image King Nebuchadnezzar saw in his dream. The two feet will touch the ground when the anti-Christ is incarnated as the man of sin, sits in the Third Temple in Jerusalem, and wants to be exalted and worshipped by man as God (2 Thessalonians 2:4), and Jesus Christ will come and destroy it in a final battle between the forces of light and darkness. But first, the spirit of the anti-Christ must incarnate as the man of sin. As discussed in Chapter 3, the birth of Zionism has opened a portal through which the deep state can actively create a condition on Earth when the anti-Christ can incarnate as the man of sin and live among humans. The end game is to build a temple in Jerusalem, which will be the epicentre of the final act of deception by the cosmic forces.

Temple Mount Faithful is an extreme Orthodox Jewish movement based in Jerusalem that is dedicated to rebuilding the Third Jewish Temple on the Temple Mount in Jerusalem and re-instituting the practice of ritual sacrifice. The movement was established in 1967, but in recent years, it has become more apocalyptic and messianic, and the restoration of the Jewish Temple has become one of its central goals. The movement has close links with Christian fundamentalist circles and is given financial support by some Christian groups. [31] The Temple Institute is preparing a blueprint for the construction of the Temple. This includes the breastplates containing precious stones of the tribes of Israel, the musical instruments of the Levitical choir, and priestly garments. [32] The date for the construction of the Third Temple is not yet set, but it will likely cause major upheaval and international crisis, starting in the Middle East and spreading beyond.

What will happen when the Third Temple is rebuilt?

Satan, the hater of all that is good, saw Adam and Eve seeking God and praying with eager hearts. He transformed his hosts into light, and the hosts started to sing praise. Satan intended to deceive Adam and Eve into believing that the light was from heaven and that his hosts were angels that God had sent to watch over them and give them light in the darkness. Satan expected that when Adam and Eve saw him and his hosts, they would bow to him, and he would overcome them before God. Adam and Eve saw the great light and heard the songs of praise, thinking it was real. God warned them that Satan had come to them in the likeness of an angel of light to be worshipped and enslave them in the presence of God. God stripped Satan of the false image he had assumed and returned him to his hideous form. Satan is the master of disguise and deceit. [2]

The mainstream media covers the current crisis in the Middle East regarding the Israel-Palestine conflict. Some believe that Israel may be wiped out by its adversaries in a major regional military conflict. There is no military power or coalition of nations that can wage war against the State of Israel and succeed. No attempt by any individual or group of nations can ever destroy the Zionism that has been in the making for the last two millennia because of the intense Christian persecution of the Jews. The Zionist portal is open, and the destiny of Israel and the world is decided by the forces of the deep state, which are far superior in resources to those that humanity can master. Moreover, there will be no multipolar world, as is often mentioned in the media. The rising new world order will serve the deep state and be single-polar, which is a prerequisite for the coming of the man of sin. The Catholic Church and the State of Israel will form important components in the composition and outlook of the new world order. The world is being transformed into a single entity to oppose God and Christ, and major regional and global conflicts must yet take place to complete the transformation. But first, the new world order must replace the existing one. It will have a leader, an administrative government, a set of laws, and an army that will act against God and the gospel of Christ.

The unfolding events in the Middle East are very troubling, and the conflict will likely spread and become a world war. The State of Israel is central to God's salvation plan, and if it were destroyed for any reason or by any force, the plan would remain unaccomplished and God's work in Christ nullified. So, despite all the hate and hostility, Israel is an important piece of the jigsaw of human redemption and will be preserved until the Third Temple is rebuilt in Jerusalem. We may expect a greater Israel to emerge from the current crisis with a wider border, but for now, we are at the beginning of what the Bible terms the birth pain. When the Third Temple is rebuilt, and the man of sin sits in the Temple, Satan and his hosts will be masquerading as light and will bring healing to people, mesmerising the nations of the Earth. Jerusalem will be the stage where the cosmic forces in the universe will hypnotise the masses with light and miracles and deceive them into believing lies and acting ungodly, the likes of which humanity has never experienced before. All eyes will be on the events in Jerusalem. People will see the great light and hear the songs of praise, thinking it is real. The false image will be stripped, and the deception will be exposed to the elect. But the false light and Satan's tricks will seduce the ungodly through the man of sin. What dreadful fate awaits those who will be blinded by the glamour and deceit of Satan and his hosts?

The battle of Armageddon is the final act of God to separate light from darkness and end dualism. The Bible paints a grim picture of what will come to the Earth. "For men will be lovers of themselves, lovers of money, braggarts, arrogant, blasphemers, disobedient to parents, unthankful, unholy, without natural feeling, unyielding, slanderers, without self-control, savage, haters of good, betrayers, reckless, puffed up, lovers of pleasure rather than lovers of god, having a form of godliness but denying the power of it—even turn away from these." (2 Timothy 3:1–5)

In this situation, God will rescue the true believers from the devastating judgement coming on Earth. "For we say this to you in the word of the Lord, that we the living who remain to the coming of the Lord will not all go before those who have fallen asleep, because the Lord Himself shall come down from heaven with a commanding shout of an archangel's voice and with God's trumpet. And the dead in Christ will rise again first, and then we who remain alive will be caught up together with them in the clouds to a meeting with the Lord in the air. And, so, we will always be with the Lord. So, then, comfort each other with these words." (1 Thessalonians 4:15–18) These verses support the spiritual rapture of the church in the turbulent times ahead.

Summary

- Zionism is a portal between humanity and the deep state that is in a different dimension. It enables the deep state to directly influence and shape the events in the world. It serves the ungodly and inhuman agenda of the dark forces of the universe.

- The anti-Christ is rooted in the Catholic Church, where Christ is and will incarnate in the flesh as the man of sin when the Third Temple is rebuilt in Jerusalem.

- The deep state is creating a new world order through wars, famines, pestilence, and diseases and paves the way for the coming of the man of sin, leading to a cataclysmic end.

Chapter 5
Summary and conclusions

Biblical scholars and Christians have expressed different views about God and His relationship with humankind. One view has gained dominance in the landscape of faith and belief systems, and that is the notion of a personal God. However, a personal God does not exist because all processes that have been unfolding in the universe since the dawn of time have done so in a duality, which started when light and darkness were separated. Dualism dictates that all things must have their opposites. Hence, God's plan for human salvation had to consist of Christ coexisting with its opposite, the anti-Christ. God is bound by the principles of His creation and cannot act outside of them.

Summary

• The deep state was formed by the angelic rebellion in heaven and is rooted in the world's empires. It is through the rise and fall of empires that the deep state keeps humanity in bondage. Salvation for humankind is possible only if this bondage is broken, and Jesus Christ is the central figure in this plan.

• Since the dawn of time, the forces of light and darkness have been in conflict over the destiny of humanity. The forces of light are good and constructive, whereas the forces of darkness are bad and destructive. However, a closer analysis reveals a more rational reason behind the workings of the universe. Dualism dictates that all things must have their opposites. Therefore, absolute monotheism and full obedience to the moral law, as commanded by God in the covenant with ancient Israel, were not possible because the opposites had to occur at the same time. Dualism has no respect for the will of God and restricts God's freedom in dealing with humankind. Since God's actions, like all other things, are subject to the uncompromising dictates of dualism, belief in a personal God cannot be justified. When belief in a personal God diminishes, what should our relationship with an impersonal God be?

• The Christianisation of the Roman Empire and the rise of the Catholic Church introduced Christ into the Empire, and dualism dictated that the opposite, the anti-Christ, should also appear in the Church. The Christian persecution of the Jews led to the birth of Zionism, which has provided a portal for the deep state to control the events directly and prepare the way for the incarnation of the anti-Christ as the man of sin. A Third Temple in Jerusalem must be rebuilt where the man of sin will sit, oppose, and exalt himself above every so-called god or object of worship. The Bible teaches that salvation is of the Jews. (John 4:22) When this verse is examined against the two legs that appeared in the image King Nebuchadnezzar of Babylon saw in his dream and Daniel the prophet interpreted, a clear meaning emerges. The two legs are two Israels. One is the Church (the redeeming Israel), where the spirit of Christ dwells, and the other is the unredeemed Israel, where Zionism and the Third Temple are. For the first foot to touch the ground, the Third Temple in Jerusalem must be rebuilt for the man of sin to come, and then the second foot will touch the ground when Jesus Christ returns to destroy the man of sin and end the reign of the empires in a final battle, Armageddon, between good and evil. Dualism will end in the final battle, and the bondage will be broken. This will be followed by the purification of the righteous in Christ and the establishment of the Kingdom of God on a new Earth, with the golden Jerusalem at its centre. Jesus Christ will be the King of the Kingdom of God.

• The gospel of Christ promises salvation to the righteous. (Psalms 37:29) The destruction of the forces of hostility towards God and humanity as defined in the deep state and the purification of the soul through Jesus Christ are central to God's scheme of salvation. The former is being achieved through Zionism, the rebuilding of the Third Temple in Jerusalem, and the coming of the man of sin, and the latter in the Church.

Conclusions

• Dualism denies the notion of a personal God.

• The spirit of the anti-Christ co-exists with the spirit of Jesus Christ in the Roman Catholic Church and is controlled by the deep state. The agenda is to destroy and remove humankind from the Earth and capture it for Satan and his hosts.

• The spirit of the anti-Christ will incarnate as the man of sin and will sit in the Third Temple in Jerusalem. This will be the final act of abomination against God.

• The new world order is being shaped by the deep state with the specific aim of paving the way for the incarnation of the anti-Christ as the man of sin.

• The forces of darkness will be destroyed in a final battle when Jesus Christ returns. This will be the battle of Armageddon, which will start in the Middle East and spread world wide.

In the dualism of light and darkness, everything has come into existence by its own accord and has the opposite. The rigid rules governing dualism cannot be suspended or superseded by the will of God or human interference. God is either in dualism or outside it. If the former is true, then God's actions are restricted by the rigid rules of dualism, but if the latter is true, then God can only rely on humans as the main agents of change and redemption. Humans are the product of duality, are enslaved to its uncompromising principles, and can never fully comply with God's command to be monotheists and obey His moral law. This being so, then, how can belief in a personal God or free will for humans be justified? We have as much free will as God had the freedom to shape the destiny of ancient Israel into a model nation.

The deep state has emerged due to the angelic rebellion in heaven. The primary objective of God's salvation plan is to defeat the deep state, even if it means giving up humanity to the violent impulses of history.

The universe is full of mysteries and marvels. But one stands out above all. It is a wonder of all wonders that humans still believe in God, praise, and glorify His name despite all the evidence suggesting that their faith and goodwill have no impact on their immediate conditions or the predicament they are in. The Lord God's relationship with humanity is marked by this greatest mystery.

Humans are often reminded of their sinful nature, shortcomings, and the need to beg for mercy and forgiveness from God. But they are never told why they should feel guilty and shameful for their actions if they have never had a say in their conception and constitution. Where is justice in all this?

There is a saying that patience is a virtue. Faith in the Lord God amidst darkness is a virtue too. The faithful are so immersed in their daily struggles that they no longer realise how noble and precious they are in the sight of God, despite all their failures. Without faith, life is a great gift that is wasted.

How has humanity managed to endure centuries of insecurity, uncertainty, suffering, war, and bloodshed? By creating and believing in stories that are based on fantasies, wishful thinking, misguided wisdom, and mythology, rather than truth.

As Jesus said, "Let one who seeks not stop seeking until that person finds; and upon finding, the person will be disturbed; and being disturbed, will be astounded; and will reign over the entirety." [1]

But would knowing the truth have helped?

When dualism prevented God from redeeming humankind by building a model nation through a covenant with ancient Israel, He resorted to monism to save His people. In Jesus Christ, dualism was dissolved and replaced by monism. The sick were healed, the dead were resurrected, and the sinners were forgiven. Monism saves the soul, and God's mercy takes us to it. Salvation cannot be achieved through any religion, religious belief, dogmatic ideas, or ritual.

The race to Jerusalem began when God separated light from darkness. Who would arrive in Jerusalem first? Light or darkness? The race has been won by darkness. What is the future of Jerusalem?

Why pray for the dead if we cannot pray for those who never lived? Pity the living and envy those who never lived.

There is a truth in the Bible that is secure in Jesus Christ, and only a few will discover it, with God's permission. It transcends God, humans, and the universe itself. Knowing that it will transform the faith of an individual.

God's providence in the person of Jesus Christ

The deep state lives in the rise and fall of the world's empires.

↓

The Christianisation of the Roman Empire added Christ to the Empire.

↓

The spirit of the anti-Christ emerged as the opposite to Christ in the Empire after the Christianisation.

↓

The Roman Empire has the duality of Christ and anti-Christ.

↓

The anti-Christ incarnates as the man of sin through the Zionist portal.

↓

The spiritual rapture of the righteous occurs.

↓

Jesus Christ returns and destroys the man of sin.

↓

The righteous are redeemed in Jesus Christ, and the kingdom of God arrives.

↓

The kingdom of light and the kingdom of darkness are separated for all eternity.

References

1. B. Layton. The Gnostic Scriptures. SCM Press Ltd, London, 1987.(ISBN: 0-334-02022-0)

2. J. B. Lumpkin. The Books of Enoch, The Angels, The Watchers and The Nephilim.
Fifth Estate Publishers USA, 2011. 2nd Edition. (ISBN: 9781936533077).

3. W. H. McNeill. A World History. Oxford University Press, Inc. 1979. (ISBN: 0 19 215860 0)

4. https://en.wikipedia.org/wiki/List_of_empires
Date visited: 21-July-2024

5. https://archive.globalpolicy.org/component/content/article/155-history/25992-empires-in-world-history.html
Date visited: 23-July-2024

6. https://www.britannica.com/place/Babylonia
Date visited: 23-July-2024

7. https://en.wikipedia.org/wiki/Siege_of_Jerusalem_(587_BC) Date visited: 23-July-2024

8. Achaemenid Empire@ Captivatinghistory.com/e-book9

9. https://en.wikipedia.org/wiki/Achaemenid_Empire
Date accessed 15/07/2020

10. https://www.rferl.org/a/1094279.html
Date visited: 23-July-2024

11. https://en.wikipedia.org/wiki/Achaemenid_destruction_of_Athens
Date visited: 24-July-2024

12. https://www.natgeokids.com/uk/discover/history/greece/10-facts-about-the-ancient-greeks/
    Date visited: 24-July-2024

13. https://www.thenational.academy/teachers/programmes/history-primary-ks2/units/ancient-greek-civilisation-why-is-alexander-called-the-great/lessons/alexanders-achievements#slide-deck
    Date visited: 26-July-2024

14. https://www.britannica.com/summary/Alexander-the-Greats-Achievements
    Date visited: 26-July-2024

15. Simon Baker. Ancient Rome. The rise and fall of an empire. Glays Ltd, Elcograf S.p.A, 2007.

16. https://en.wikipedia.org/wiki/First_Jewish%E2%80%93Roman_War
    Date visited: 24-July-2024

17. https://cissm.umd.edu/research-impact/publications/deaths-wars-and-conflicts-20th-century
    Date visited: 24-July-2024

18. https://www.theguardian.com/education/higher/humanities/partner/story/0,9885,678228,00.html
    Date visited: 06-August 2014

19. https://en.wikipedia.org/wiki/List_of_Catholic_saints
    Date visited: 01-August-2024

20. R. Montgomery and B. O'Dell. The List. Persecution of Jews by Christians throughout history. Root Source Press. Jerusalem, Israel 2019.
    (ISBN: 978-965-7738-13-9)

21. https://en.wikipedia.org/wiki/History_of_the_Byzantine_Empire
    Date visited: 29-July-2024

22. J. J. Norwich. Byzantium. The decline and fall. Viking. The

Penguin Group. 1995.(ISBN: 0-670-82377-5)

23. https://reviews.history.ac.uk/review/371/
    Date visited: 30-July-2024

24. https://www.britannica.com/topic/Russian-Orthodox-Church
    Date visited: 06-August-2024

25. https://en.wikipedia.org/wiki/Second_Vatican_Council
    Date visited: 06-August-2024

26. A. Callinicos. The Revolutionary ideas of Marx. Bookmarks. London 1993.(ISBN: 0 906224 09 8)

27. https://en.wikipedia.org/wiki/History_of_the_Russian_Orthodox_Church
    Date visited: 04-09-2024

28. https://scottmanning.com/content/communist-body-count/
    Date visited: 04-August-2024

29. T. Childers. The third Reich – A history of Nazi Germany. Simon & Schuster. New York. 2017 (ISBN: 978-1-4516-5113-3), ((ISBN: 978-1-4516-5115-7) (ebook)

30. https://history.state.gov/milestones/1945-1952/creation-israel
    Date visited: 05-August-2024

31. https://en.wikipedia.org/wiki/Temple_Mount_Faithful
    Date visited: 31-July-2024

32. https://free.messianicbible.com/feature/israels-priests-prepare-third-temple/
    Date visited: 01-August-2024

All scripture quotations have been taken from the Interlinear Bible, Hebrew-Greek- English. Jay P. Green, Sr Hendrickson Publishers, 2020. (ISBN: 978-1-56563-977-5) 8.

Afterword

The history of faith is rich with ideas, and the search for God continues unabated. The truth is somewhere amid stories, but humans are the greatest storytellers ever to live. Stories are imaginative and entertaining, but they may not always get us to the truth. The biblical narrative has generated significant interest among religious scholars and believers. The common consensus among most Christians is that there is a loving God who sacrificed His only son to save humankind from sin and damnation, and that the universe complies with the will of the creator God. This ignores the fundamental way the universe works. When light was separated from darkness, duality emerged, and in duality, all things came into existence of their own accord over a very long time and through unimaginable violence and destructive processes. Dualism dictates that everything must have an opposite. This principle is not amenable to the will of the Creator, who commands strict monotheism and full obedience to His moral law, because dualism dictates that the opposites, polytheism and disobedience, must also happen. The biblical narrative indicates a historical transition from dualism to monism. Faith in a personal God has not always been fulfilling and does not answer all the questions. How can a relationship with an impersonal God develop and be rewarding to the faithful? At times, it looks as if God is an observer, a bystander, and non-engaging in human affairs. A personal God may well be a figment of our imagination.

About the author

Dr. Ali Ansarifar has been living in the United Kingdom for over 40 years. He was awarded a bachelor's degree and a doctorate in materials science from Queen Mary College, the University of London, and a diploma in interface science from Imperial College, the University of London. He worked as a postdoctoral research assistant at Imperial College, London, and the Cavendish Laboratory, Department of Physics, University of Cambridge. He was an upper-senior research scientist in a rubber research and development centre in Hertfordshire, UK, and a lecturer in polymer engineering in the Materials Department at Loughborough University until he retired as a senior lecturer. He has given lectures, seminars, and workshops in the United States, the United Kingdom, Europe, the Middle East, and Southeast Asia. He has published over 150 books and technical research papers in peer-reviewed international scientific journals, conference papers, articles in technical magazines for the polymer and tire industries and textbooks and contributed chapters to scientific books. He has been on the editorial boards of Rubber and Adhesion scientific journals and has been awarded prizes for his scientific publications. He is a Fellow of the Higher Education Academy, UK, and a servant of Jesus Christ.

About the book

This book discusses the biblical and historical origins of the deep state and the new world order. There was light and darkness at the beginning. The angelic rebellion in heaven provided darkness with an effective means to bring humanity into bondage. The gospel of Christ offers salvation and eternal life to the faithful, and central to it is the defeat of the deep state and the emancipation of humanity from its bondage. This is being achieved through Jesus Christ, the birth of Zionism, and the establishment of the State of Israel in the Middle East. The unfolding events in the Middle East are in line with the biblical prophecies and are occurring within the framework that the Lord God put in place after the birth of Jesus Christ. The book sheds light on the timeline and the processes that are taking place to bring the world to its conclusion. The future events in the Holy Land will be cosmic, and the Catholic Church will play a major role.

Final notes by the author

In today's discourse and media frenzy, the terms "deep state" and "new world order" appear frequently. However, these terms are often misunderstood. A Christian view of history will help to clarify this misconception. The deep state is Satan and his hosts, who serve the dark forces of the universe, and their agenda is to destroy humankind and inherit the Earth. The new world order is a world that is being shaped by the deep state for the specific purpose of the coming of the man of sin. The deep state is rooted in the rise and fall of the world's empires, and humankind is in bondage to it. To emancipate humanity from this bondage, God Christianised the Roman Empire and introduced Christ. Dualism dictated that the opposite, the anti-Christ, must exist too. In the final act, the anti-Christ must incarnate into the man of sin. The birth of Zionism opened a portal for the deep state to operate in human affairs through the anti-Christ and prepare the way for the coming of the man of sin. The next stage is the rebuilding of the Third Temple in Jerusalem for the man of sin to appear in the flesh. Jesus will then return and destroy the man of sin in a cosmic battle known as Armageddon. The final act is according to Daniel's interpretation of King Nebuchadnezzar's dream, in which he saw a figure with two legs but no feet. The feet will touch the ground when the man of sin and Jesus Christ come to Earth for the final battle, the reign of the empires will end, and humanity's redemption will commence. So, expect wars, destruction, and mayhem to come to Earth on an unimaginably vast scale. The faithful in Christ have no fear because the Lord God has secured their salvation and will soon be heading to the bridal chamber.

Books by the author

1. Sharing the Faith. Kingdom Publishers, London, UK. 2021. ISBN: 978-1-913247-54-6

2. The Bible Story of Mankind. A Covenant with God with no Get-out Clause. Balboa Press, UK. 2021. ISBN: 978-1-9822-8394-0 (sc). ISBN: 978-1-9822-8393-3 (e).

3. Why Did God Create Mankind? The Problem of Duality with God. Balboa Press, UK. 2021. ISBN: 978-1-9822-8439-8 (sc). ISBN: 978-1-9822-8440-4 (e).

4. The British and American Empires and the State of Israel. Until the Kingdom of God Comes. Kingdom Publishers, London, UK. 2022. ISBN: 978-1-913247-98-0

5. The March to the Armageddon, Balboa Press, UK 2022. ISBN: 978-1-9822-8377-3 (sc), ISBN: 978-1-9822-8378-0(e)

6. How Did God Create Mankind? Scientific and Biblical Views. Kingdom Publishers, London, UK. 2022. ISBN: 978-1-911697-64-0

7. Why does Judaism reject Jesus Christ? Unintended Messianic expectations and unplanned temple-worship. Kingdom Publishers, London, UK. 2023. ISBN: 978-1-911697-73-2

8. A Brief History of the World – The Great Deception. Kingdom Publishers, London, UK. 2024. ISBN: 978-1-916801-01-1

www.ingramcontent.com/pod-product-compliance
Lightning Source LLC
Chambersburg PA
CBHW061225070526
44584CB00029B/3987